A Special Type of
Neighbourhood

Rob Waring, *Series Editor*

T0354112

HEINLE
CENGAGE Learning

Australia • Brazil • Japan • Korea • Mexico • Singapore • Spain • United Kingdom • United States

Words to Know

This story is set in the United States (U.S.), in the state of California. It takes place in the city of San Francisco. [sæn frənsɪskoʊ]

 A Multicultural Neighbourhood. Read the paragraph. Then complete the sentences with the correct form of the underlined words.

    This story is about an old neighbourhood in San Francisco called the Mission District or The Mission for short. This neighbourhood started near a church called Mission Dolores. Spanish missionaries started the church in 1791. They wanted to teach people about their beliefs. Now, many people from other countries live in The Mission. The majority of these immigrants are Latino. They come from Central and South America. This has made the community that lives in the area very multicultural.

1. An area of a town is called a n_____.
2. People who travel around and teach about their god are m_____.
3. A place where people pray to a god is a c_____.
4. Something that is related to traditions and beliefs from many different countries is m_____.
5. A group of people who live in the same area form a c_____.
6. People who move to another country to live are i_____.
7. People from Central or South America are also known as L_____.

B Things to Do in the Mission District. Here are some different activities people do in the Mission District. Write the letter of each phrase next to the correct activity.

a. sing in the choir   **c.** play music
b. paint murals   **d.** eat Latin-American food

San Francisco's Mission Dolores church was built in 1791.

E very Sunday, people can hear the music of the Mission Dolores church in San Francisco. With this sound comes memories of the Spanish missionaries who built the church in 1791. They didn't know it at the time, but it was the start of a special type of neighbourhood: the Mission District.

The Mission is a place with a long and varied history. One member of the community describes it as a central part of San Francisco, because it's near where the city began long ago. He adds that it's important for people to understand the many levels of history in the neighbourhood. He feels that this knowledge is a big part of understanding what it means to be a real San Franciscan.

Fact Check: True or false?

1. The Mission District started in 1791.

2. Spanish missionaries built the church.

3. The Mission District has many layers of history.

One of the most interesting parts of the Mission District is its people. Over the years, immigrants have come to the area from Ireland, Germany and Italy. But the most recent immigrants are mainly from Mexico and other countries in Central and South America. It's easy to see the style that these recent additions give the neighbourhood. You can see it in the art on the walls, taste it in the food and hear it in the music.

Juan Pedro Gaffney grew up in the Mission District. He's the director of the Spanish Choir of San Francisco. In the past, his group has performed to raise money for people after **natural disasters**[1] in Central America. Many people in the choir are very close to these countries. Juan Pedro explains that the people in the Mission District share the pain and the happiness of their friends and relatives in Latin America. He says that the local community feels a sense of common involvement. They really care when a neighbouring nation is in pain.

---

[1]**natural disaster:** natural event that causes a lot of damage and serious problems

During happy and sad times, the music produced in The Mission deeply affects everyone. Sometimes it helps people to share their sadness. Sometimes it helps them to enjoy life. Juan Pedro explains that music has always been an important part of the **cultural identity**[2] in The Mission. He feels that the music of the district is colourful and lively. According to him, it's absolutely "**jumping**".[3]

It isn't just the music that's colourful and lively in the Mission District. The art of The Mission is full of life as well.

---

[2] **cultural identity:** sense of closeness to one's culture and environment

[3] **jumping:** (slang) fun and energetic

Canción como un Disparo, Como un Libro
á, una "...rilla. Como D. y el Amor"
"...te Like a Book,
& Love."

The local art community in The Mission stays close to the area's culture and tradition. A local art organisation often leads people on walks through the district. They visit streets like Balmy Alley, which is famous for its murals.

Artist Ray Patlan talks about the art of the Mission District. "What happens is, the murals begin to reflect the community itself", he says. In 1984, Patlan helped to organise a group of artists to paint a series of murals here. The theme at the time was 'Peace in Central America'.

Nowadays, however, while the district remains mainly Latino, it is no longer 1984. The political situation is no longer the same. Patlan points out that both politics and the world have changed over the years. He then adds that because of this, the art in The Mission has changed as well. He explains that the art in the area is part of the streets, and it's also a reflection of the community. So, as the community changes, people can see changes in the murals as well.

Even though the meanings behind the murals are always changing, they are still very powerful. Apparently, they're something the community likes a lot. Andrea Coombes lives in The Mission. "It's great," she says. "It's like coming home to a piece of art every day. Every time we drive up it's just very **vibrant**." [4]

[4] **vibrant:** lively and interesting

The artists have strong feelings about the work they produce. One artist explains that the artists in The Mission are fighting for fairness in the community. They're also fighting to help the environment. Here in the Mission District, these groups of artists maintain their cultural identity in traditional San Francisco style!

Many of these artists feel that The Mission is a successful neighbourhood where new immigrants are welcome. "People see that they're not so different from each other," says one artist. "There [are] a lot of things that **bind**[5] [the immigrants] through culture and tradition."

---

[5]**bind:** unite; bring together

The members of Saint Peter's Church are another group that understands the closeness between culture and tradition. Mission Dolores was the **foundation**[6] of the Mission District, but Saint Peter's is another strong base in the area.

Father Dan McGuire is the leader of Saint Peter's. He talks about all of the different cultures that form the community around the church. "The beauty of this particular **parish**,"[7] says Father McGuire, "is that the different cultures from Latin America and the different countries of Latin America come together here. And they really form a common unity." The people who go to this church are from countries such as Mexico, El Salvador, and Peru. They come from all over Latin America.

---

[6]**foundation:** starting point; base
[7]**parish:** an area that has its own church

SAN FRANCISCO
(MISSION DOLORES)
CALIFORNIA

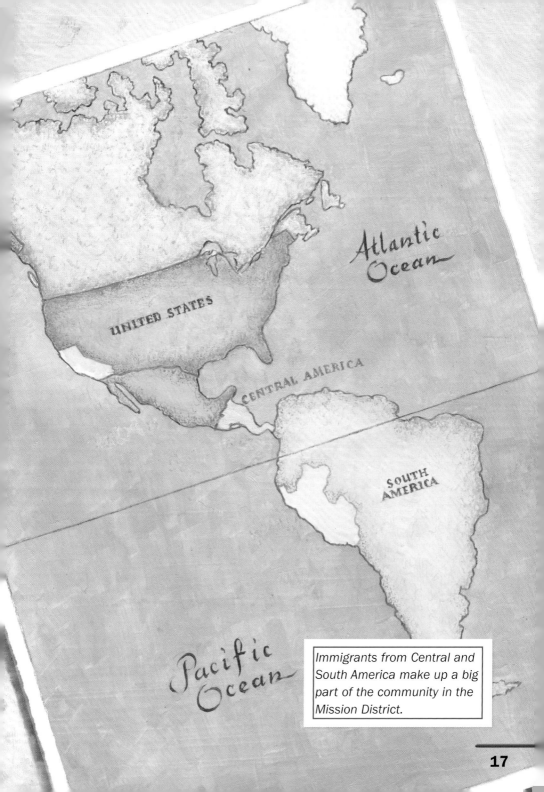

Atlantic Ocean

UNITED STATES

CENTRAL AMERICA

SOUTH AMERICA

Pacific Ocean

Immigrants from Central and South America make up a big part of the community in the Mission District.

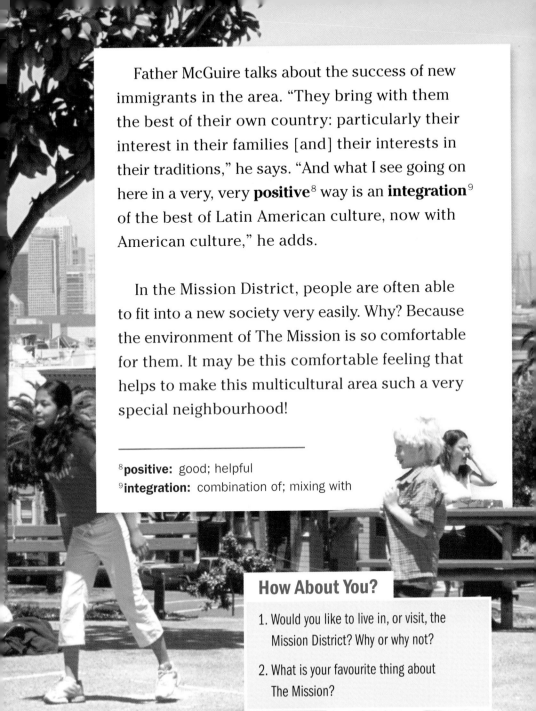

Father McGuire talks about the success of new immigrants in the area. "They bring with them the best of their own country: particularly their interest in their families [and] their interests in their traditions," he says. "And what I see going on here in a very, very **positive**[8] way is an **integration**[9] of the best of Latin American culture, now with American culture," he adds.

In the Mission District, people are often able to fit into a new society very easily. Why? Because the environment of The Mission is so comfortable for them. It may be this comfortable feeling that helps to make this multicultural area such a very special neighbourhood!

---

[8]**positive:** good; helpful
[9]**integration:** combination of; mixing with

How About You?

1. Would you like to live in, or visit, the Mission District? Why or why not?

2. What is your favourite thing about The Mission?

After You Read

1. The Mission District is a lively area of San Francisco.
    A. True
    B. False

2. On page 5, 'they' in paragraph one refers to:
    A. people at church on Sunday
    B. missionaries in 1791
    C. people in Mission Delores
    D. people living in San Francisco

3. Which is a good heading for page 7?
    A. Strong Cultural Identity in Neighbourhood
    B. Juan Pedro Gaffney's German Choir
    C. Always Raising Money
    D. Juan Pedro Gaffney Moves to Area

4. On page 8, the word 'deeply' can be replaced by:
    A. really
    B. badly
    C. only
    D. lively

5. When does the music of the Mission District affect people?
    A. When they are happy
    B. When they are enjoying life
    C. When they are sad.
    D. all of the above

6. According to page 12, what does Ray Patlan think is important about the murals?
    A. They are very colourful.
    B. They were all painted in 1984.
    C. They are only about peace.
    D. They reflect the people and times.

7. On page 12, 'it's' in paragraph one refers to:
   A. politics
   B. art
   C. community
   D. music

8. A good heading for page 15 is:
   A. Mission District Artists Fight for Fairness
   B. Mission District Artists Only Fight for Environment
   C. Style Missing in Mission District
   D. New Immigrants Sometimes Welcome

9. The Mission District is a lively and interesting neighbourhood
   _____ many different people.
   A. where
   B. from
   C. in
   D. with

10. On page 16, the word 'foundation' in paragraph one can be
    replaced by:
    A. culture
    B. house
    C. base
    D. parish

11. Father Dan McGuire believes that people in the Mission District:
    A. have formed a community around the church.
    B. are only from Mexico.
    C. should always come to his parish.
    D. come from Saint Peter's.

12. Which expression best describes the Mission District?
    A. colourful
    B. loud
    C. Latino
    D. multicultural

A New Berlin

The old Berlin was known for its fine music, food and art. Its streets were full of historical buildings and there were beautiful views everywhere. However, for 28 years, from 1961 to 1989, the city was divided into East and West Berlin by the Berlin Wall. This wall separated the two areas that were controlled by different powers. During this time, Berlin lost some of its liveliness.

Nowadays, the city has many immigrant groups and a rising art and music culture. Berlin has become one of the most vibrant, multicultural cities in Europe. Today, about 3.5 million people live there. Half a million of these people were not born in Germany. These immigrants have come from 185 different countries. Many live in communities with other people from their homelands. Each of these neighbourhoods is a great place to see and each has a very different look and feel.

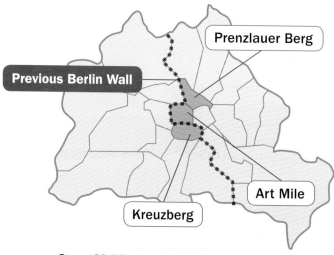

Some Multicultural Neighbourhoods in Berlin

Every year thousands of people attend Berlin's art festivals

Kreuzberg

Many people from the country of Turkey now live in the area of Kreuzberg. This is a lively area. In addition to all the special foods from Turkey and the bookshops, you will also find nightclubs here. In these clubs, people from many different cultures come together to play music and dance all night.

Art Mile

In the recent past, most artists lived and worked in West Berlin. But today everything has changed. The 'Art Mile' was an area in East Berlin that wasn't very interesting in the past. It is now the city's lively art centre. Berlin has two international art events in the 'Art Mile'. These events attract thousands of visitors from around the world every year.

Prenzlauer Berg

Visitors love the neighbourhood called Prenzlauerberg. Its streets are jumping with the energy of all the musicians, artists and designers who live and work there. But there are also quiet, restful shops where people drink tea, read books or write their own stories.

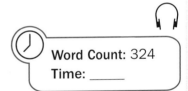

Word Count: 324
Time: _____

Vocabulary List

bind (15)

choir (3, 7)

church (2, 5, 16)

community (2, 5, 7, 11, 12, 15, 16, 17)

cultural identity (8, 15)

foundation (16)

immigrant (2, 7, 15, 17, 19)

integration (19)

jumping (8)

Latino (2, 12)

missionaries (2, 5)

multicultural (2, 19)

mural (3, 11, 12)

music (3, 5, 7, 8)

natural disaster (7)

neighbourhood (2, 5, 7, 15, 16, 19)

parish (16)

positive (19)

vibrant (12)